This book donated to your public library by the Oregon Coast Agate Club

THE BEST BOOK OF

Fossils, Rocks, and Minerals

Chris Pellant

KINGFISHER

BOSTON

Contents

KINGFISHER

a Houghton Mifflin Company imprint
222 Berkeley Street
Boston, Massachusetts 02116
www.houghtonmifflinbooks.com

Author: Chris Pellant
Series editor: Camilla Reid
Editor: Emma Wild
Designer: John Jamieson
Illustrators: Ray Grinaway,
    Chris Forsey

First published in 2000
10 9

9TR/0406/WKT/MA(MA)/128MA/F

Copyright © Kingfisher Publications Plc 2000

LIBRARY OF CONGRESS
CATALOGING-IN-PUBLICATION DATA
Pellant, Chris.
  My best book of fossils, rocks, and minerals /
Chris Pellant.
    p. cm.
  Includes index.
  Summary: Briefly describes different kinds of rocks
and minerals, telling how they are formed, where
they are found and their uses and examines what
we can learn from fossils.
  ISBN 0-7534-5274-X
  1. Fossils—Juvenile literature. 2. Rocks—Juvenile
literature. 3. Minerals—Juvenile literature.
[1. Rocks. 2. Fossils. 3. Minerals.] I. Title.

QE714.5 .P44 2000
560—dc21   99-044104

ISBN 0-7534-5274-X
ISBN 978-07534-5274-5

Printed in China

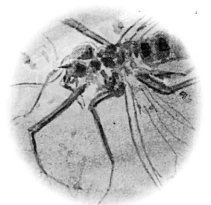

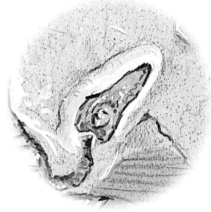

The age of the Earth

Our rocky planet is older than we could ever imagine. About 4,600 million years ago, the Earth was a huge, fiery ball circling the sun. Much of the surface was covered with hot, liquid rock—lava that poured out from volcanoes and meteorites that had crashed down from space.

Cooling down

Over millions of years, the surface began to cool and shrink. Inside the Earth, chemical substances called minerals joined together to make different kinds of rocks. A rocky crust formed on the outside. Today, the Earth's surface seems solid, but new rocks are constantly forming.

Our rocky world

The rocks that we see today on the Earth's surface were formed in different ways. Geologists have discovered that all rocks belong to three main groups: sedimentary, igneous, and metamorphic. The names describe how the rocks were made—sedimentary means "made from sediment," igneous means "fiery," and metamorphic means "changed."

Crust

Mantle

Liquid core

Solid core

Under our feet

The Earth has a hard rocky crust. Below the crust lies the mantle, which is so hot that in some places the rock has melted. The core is even hotter and is made of both solid and liquid metal.

Made by fire

Many igneous rocks form when lava is forced out of an erupting volcano, and then cools and hardens on the surface.

Layers of sediment

Sedimentary rocks are made
from sediments such as sand,
clay, and seashells that pile
up in layers in lakes, rivers,
and oceans. Over time, these
layers are pressed tightly
together to make solid rock.

Sedimentary rock layers in cliffs

Metamorphic rocks form mountains

Changed rocks

Metamorphic rocks form
in the ground when heat and
pressure change the structure
and appearance of igneous
and sedimentary rocks. The
changed rocks are pushed
up from under the ground
to form hills and mountains.

Nature's beauty

The Earth has many beautiful and dramatic landscapes. Every valley, hill, and mountain is carved out of rock. Yet landscapes change constantly as rivers, glaciers, and the sea wear away the rocks.

Deep valley

Over thousands of years, the rushing waters of the Colorado River have cut through rock to form the Grand Canyon. Layers of sedimentary rock can clearly be seen running across the sides of the canyon.

Giant steps

Giant's Causeway in Northern Ireland is made from igneous rock. As this volcanic rock cooled, it shrank and cracked to form thousands of six-sided columns. The rocks look like a giant staircase leading down to the sea.

Mighty peaks

The Alps are a high, rugged mountain range in Europe. These soaring peaks are made from metamorphoric rock that was first forced to the surface 30 million years ago. In geological terms, these mountains are still very young.

Minerals and crystals

Minerals are the natural elements and compounds in the Earth's crust that make up rocks. There are over 3,500 different minerals and many form beautiful crystals. Gemstones, salts, metals such as gold, and even talc are all different kinds of minerals. Geologists identify minerals by looking at features like color, shape, and hardness.

Crystal creation

Hot liquids rich in minerals move through the Earth's crust. As these liquids cool, the minerals grow into crystals in hollows in rocks.

Mineral quartz forms fine crystals in many colors. This purple crystal is called amethyst quartz

This amethyst has large, six-sided crystals

Color

A good way of identifying minerals is to study their color, which can be one of their most striking features. They come in a range of brilliant and vivid colors.

Shape

When crystals grow, they make many wonderful shapes. The shapes are the result of the neat arrangement of atoms and molecules inside the mineral.

Hardness

Each mineral has a certain hardness that is measured by how easily it is scratched by another object. The softest mineral is talc and the hardest is diamond.

Azurite
has blue crystals

Quartz
is hexagon-shaped

Diamond
cannot be scratched by any other object

Malachite
has green crystals

Pyrite
is cube-shaped

Fluorite
can be scratched with a blade

Realgar
has red crystals

Barite
has flat oblongs

Calcite
can be scratched with a coin

Galena
has gray crystals

Hematite
is kidney-shaped

Talc
can be scratched with a fingernail

Minerals at work

Throughout history, people have dug up minerals and rocks from the ground and used them to make many everyday objects. The discovery of metals and other raw materials changed the way people lived. Valuable metals, called ores, were found in rocks. Many items can be made by using mixtures of metals, or alloys.

Ancient alloy

Bronze is a mixture of tin and copper. It is strong and hard-wearing. This food container was made in China around 3000 B.C.

Roman metal

The Romans used lead for making their water pipes because it was very easy to bend. They heated the ore to extract the pure metal.

Renaissance color

During the Renaissance, painters crushed up brightly colored minerals to make pigments. They mixed these with oil to make paints.

Writing material

When we write with a pencil, we are using a mineral. The thin black material in a pencil is called graphite.

The aluminum can story

1 Aluminum is a light, easily-shaped metal. It comes from an ore called bauxite, which is dug out of huge quarries. The ore is then taken to a refining factory to remove the metal.

2 In order to remove the aluminum from the ore, the raw bauxite is heated beyond its melting point. This is called smelting. The melted aluminum is made into flat sheets of metal.

3 At another factory, the aluminum goes through further changes. Gradually, the sheets of metal are made into thousands of small cans that are used for holding drinks and food.

4 The Earth contains enough bauxite to last for the next 300 years. However, melting down scrap aluminum is much cheaper than mining it. Collect and recycle as many used cans as possible.

Precious gemstones

Gemstones are formed from minerals inside the Earth's crust. When rough gems are cut and polished they become very beautiful and valuable objects. For thousands of years, people have worn gems because of their amazing color, special shape, and dazzling beauty. Some of the rarest and most precious jewels are diamonds, rubies, sapphires, and emeralds.

The Imperial State Crown is part of the British crown jewels. It is worn by the queen, Elizabeth II, for special royal events.

Royal jewels

There are over 3,000 precious gemstones set in the British Imperial State Crown. In the center of the crown is a large red ruby. Below it is the Cullinan II diamond. It is part of the largest diamond ever found. The crown also contains many deep green emeralds, blue sapphires, and shiny pearls. It is very heavy—it weighs over two pounds.

In the raw

Gems found in rocks look a little dull in their natural state. Experts cut them out of the rock, and then shape and polish them until they sparkle and shine.

Gemstone in rock

Rough gemstone

Glittering jewel

Turquoise
December

Garnet
January

Amethyst
February

Topaz
November

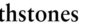

Opal
October

Birthstones

People sometimes wear a special gemstone called a birthstone in a piece of jewelry. The stone shows in what month of the year a person was born. People also believe that birthstones bring good luck to the wearer.

Aquamarine
March

Diamond
April

Sapphire
September

Emerald
May

Peridot
August

Ruby
July

Pearl
June

15

Fascinating fossils

How fossils form

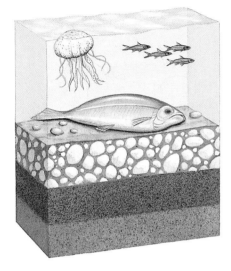

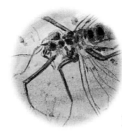

Fossils are the remains, or traces, of long-dead animals and plants, and can be millions of years old. Most fossils are discovered in sedimentary rock, in areas that were once in or near water, such as seas or rivers. They were formed after prehistoric plants and animals died and were buried under layers of sediment. While the soft parts rotted away, the hard parts, such as shells, bones, teeth, and even whole skeletons, became fossils.

1 When a fish dies, its body sinks to the seabed. The soft parts of the fish rot away.

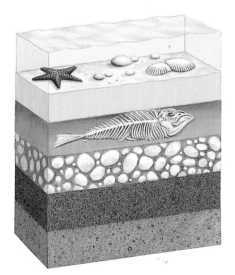

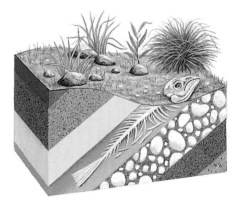

2 Gradually, the skeleton is covered with layers of sand and mud. This settles and becomes solid rock.

3 After millions of years, movements in the Earth bring the rocks containing the fossil above sea level.

4 The rocks containing the fossil are worn away by the weather and the fossil is exposed on land.

Frozen in time

Not all fossils are found
in stone. Some plants and
animals are found as they
were in life. There are many
different ways in which
fossils can be preserved.

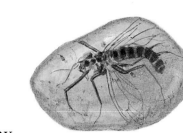

Insects can be
preserved whole
in pine-tree resin.
Over time, this
turns into amber

The wood of this tree
trunk has been replaced,
molecule by molecule,
by minerals that
turned to stone.
This is called
petrification

This ancient leaf
imprint is nearly
300 million years
old. The original
leaf was fossilized
in layers of coal

Ice can preserve
bodies. This baby
mammoth was
found frozen in
the ice in Siberia,
in Russia

This detailed
fossil of an early
fish has been
preserved in stone

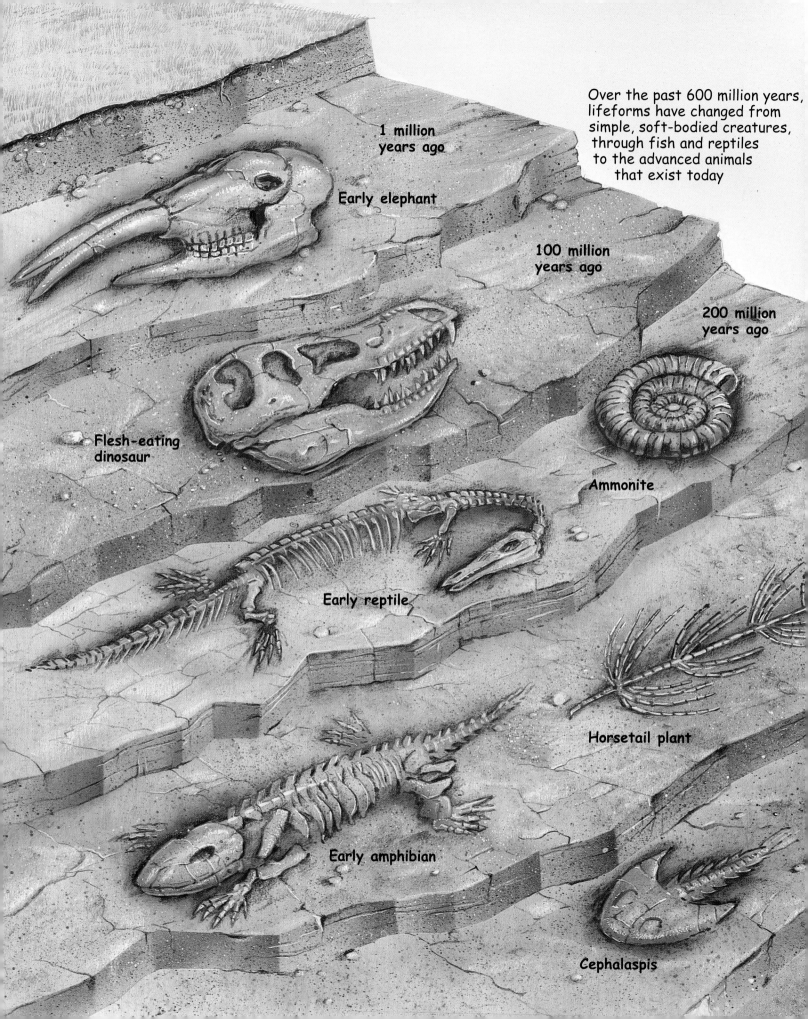

Over the past 600 million years,
lifeforms have changed from
simple, soft-bodied creatures,
through fish and reptiles
to the advanced animals
that exist today

1 million
years ago

Early elephant

100 million
years ago

200 million
years ago

Flesh-eating
dinosaur

Ammonite

Early reptile

Horsetail plant

Early amphibian

Cephalaspis

Layers of life

Millions of living things have existed on Earth, but only a small number of them ever became fossils.

Fossils are very important because they show how life on our planet has changed over many millions of years.

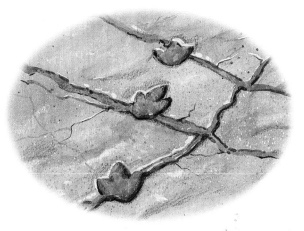

Dinosaur footprints in the rock

Dating the Earth

The Earth's history is divided into periods. Different creatures and plants lived at different times. Geologists can tell how old rocks are by studying the kinds of fossils that are found in them.

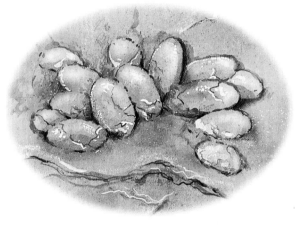

Dinosaur eggs found in China

Trace fossils

Fossils that show where animals have been are called trace fossils. Many large dinosaurs left fossilized footprints and eggs as evidence of where they once lived.

300 million years ago

400 million years ago

Early fish

500 million years ago

Trilobite

Brachiopod

600 million years ago

Ediacaran animal

Clues to the past

Evolution is the way in which animals and plants change over many generations. Fossils are clues about how life on Earth has evolved. They show us the links between many of today's species and their long-extinct ancestors. For example, by studying the *Archaeopteryx* fossils found in Germany, scientists discovered more about the ancient link between birds and reptiles.

Clawed climber

Archaeopteryx spent much of its time in trees, using the sharp claws on its feet and wings to climb.

A pair of
Archaeopteryx
climb above
the treetops

Archaeopteryx had razorlike teeth, ideal for eating prey like dragonflies

Winged wonder

Archaeopteryx was a poor flier and would have used its wide wings to glide from branch to branch or to swoop to the ground.

Missing link

In 1861, the discovery of the first *Archaeopteryx* fossil amazed scientists. They believed that it was the remains of a bird because it had feathers and wings. But it also had some reptilelike features such as sharp teeth, claws, scaly legs, and a long, bony tail. For the first time, a possible link between reptiles and birds had been found.

Fossil hunters

Discovering a new dinosaur site is an exciting event. The remains of these creatures have been found in remote places as far apart as the United States, China, Australia, and Britain. Occasionally, people have stumbled across dinosaur bones by accident. More often, the bones are found by geologists who know where to look.

Dinosaur dig

When a skeleton is unearthed, it has to be moved carefully because the bones are very fragile. The remains are then taken to a museum to be studied and put on display.

A brush is used to remove dust and sand from around the fossil

The bones are wrapped up to keep them from getting damaged

She sells seashells

This tongue twister is about Mary Anning, a young English fossil hunter. Early in the 1800s, she discovered the skeleton of an ichthyosaur near the sea in England. This was one of the first fossils of this marine reptile ever to be found, and she sold it for a large amount of money.

The geologists wear protective clothing and hard hats at all times while on the site

Rock is carefully removed from around the skeleton using special tools

A detailed drawing is made to show exactly where the bones were discovered

Fossil fuels

Coal, oil, and natural gas are all fossil fuels, and supply the energy we use to power our cars, homes, and schools. They are formed from ancient plants and animals, and are found in underground rocks. Coal is made from fossilized plants, while oil is made from the remains of tiny sea creatures that lived millions of years ago.

Excess gas burning off

How coal forms

1 Millions of years ago, huge swampy forests covered the Earth. As the giant trees and plants died, they fell onto the wet forest floor. They were covered by mud and began to rot.

2 Gradually, the plant remains were buried under more layers of rock and mud. Over millions of years, they turned into peat, and eventually into hard, black coal.

3 The coal lies in deep, underground seams. To reach it, a shaft is dug down to the layer of coal. A horizontal tunnel is drilled along the seam and the coal is brought to the surface.

Oil rig

An oil rig is a platform fixed to the seabed that drills into the rocks below and pumps up the oil. The oil is then sent down pipelines to land where it is made into gasoline and other products.

Helicopter

Crane

Heliport

Lifeboat

Stabilizing leg attached to the seabed

Starting a collection

The best way to learn about fossils, rocks, and minerals is to start your own collection. Keep an eye out for new specimens near beaches, cliffs, and other places where rocks are exposed. Try to find an interesting rock in every place you visit.

Eager explorers

Beaches are great places to hunt for rocks and fossils. Fossils are exposed as the wind and waves wash away soil and plants and break up the rocks. Do not damage or disturb the sites you visit and don't take too many fossils. Always leave something of interest for other collectors to find. Remember to tell an adult before you go collecting.

Displaying

Once you have found some interesting rocks and fossils, clean them carefully. It is very important to make a list of the fossils you have found and where you found them. Try identifying any new finds by looking them up in a book. You can read about their history and label them with the correct names. You can put the best ones on display.

Out of this world

Look up into the clear night sky and you may be able to see bright sparks of light flying across it. These are called shooting stars and are caused by meteoroids, which are lumps of space rock left over from the birth of other planets in the solar system.

A man stands by a meteorite, a piece of space rock that has landed on Earth

Mighty meteorites

When meteoroids enter the Earth's atmosphere, they burn up in the intense heat and glow brightly. The lumps that actually reach the Earth's surface are called meteorites. Although they are extremely rare, some do strike our planet every year. Many of them crash into the oceans or remote areas like deserts.

An astronaut scoops up rock samples from the surface of the moon

Anorthosite   **Basalt**   **Breccia**

Lunar landscapes

Moon rocks collected by astronauts have provided scientists with clues about the moon's history. Tests show that the moon's rocks are similar to rocks found all over the Earth. Because of this, scientists now think that the moon may once have been part of the Earth.

Unearthing the facts

As your collection of fossils, rocks, and minerals grows, you will want to find out more. Try looking in your local library for useful books, or ask your science teacher for information. If you visit a natural history museum, there should be a collection of interesting fossils, rocks, and minerals, as well as people who can help you identify your own specimens. The more you study the Earth, the more you will realize that it is a beautiful place full of natural treasures that must all be carefully protected.

The camarasaur's long neck allowed it to reach high into trees to eat the leaves

A school class visits their local museum to look at the amazing fossils on display

Gentle giant

Dinosaurs are often the most popular part of a museum exhibition. This plant-eating *Camarasaurus* lived over 150 million years ago. Scientists can learn a lot about how these creatures lived by studying their remains.

Glossary

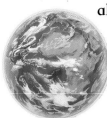

alloy A mixture of metals, or of a metal and another substance.

basalt An igneous rock that forms from hardened lava after a volcanic eruption.

bauxite The rock ore from which aluminum is refined.

bronze An alloy made from copper and tin.

canyon A very deep, narrow valley, often formed when a river cuts through rock.

compound Two or more elements joined together chemically.

core The center of the Earth, made of heavy metals.

crust The outer, rocky layer of the Earth.

crystal The special shape in which many minerals form. A crystal has fixed properties and the sides are usually flat and regular.

dinosaurs The group of now extinct reptiles that lived between 230 and 65 million years ago.

Theory of
evolution The way in which organisms change over time. Simple life forms have evolved into complex animals and plants. *Wrong*

fossil The remains, or traces, of animals and plants usually preserved in rocks.

fossil fuels The fuels coal, oil, and natural gas, all of which are formed from the remains of once-living organisms.

gemstone A mineral that is valuable because of its beauty, often worn in a piece of jewelry.

geologist Someone who studies rocks and fossils to learn more about the Earth's history.

graphite A mineral made entirely of the element carbon. Graphite is very soft and black.

lava The hot, melted rock that pours out of an erupting volcano.

magma The hot, liquid rock deep in the Earth's crust that becomes lava on the surface.

meteorite A lump of rock from outer space that hits the Earth's surface.

mineral A compound or an element that forms crystals. All rocks are made from minerals.

ore A mineral that contains valuable material such as metal.

petrified Turned to stone.

resin The sticky liquid that oozes from pine trees and hardens to form amber.

rock A mass of mineral material that may or may not be solid.

smelting The process by which a metal is removed from an ore.

31

Index